THE PEOPLE PLEASER'S RECOVERY JOURNAL

EU Representative: Macmillan Publishers Ireland Ltd,
1st Floor, The Liffey Trust Centre, 117–126 Sheriff Street
Upper, Dublin 1, D01 YC43

THE PEOPLE PLEASER'S RECOVERY JOURNAL.

Copyright © 2025 by St. Martin's Press.
All rights reserved. Printed in China.
For information, address St. Martin's Publishing Group,
120 Broadway, New York, NY 10271.

www.castlepointbooks.com

The Castle Point Books trademark is owned by
Castle Point Publishing, LLC.

Castle Point books are published and distributed by
St. Martin's Publishing Group.

Edited by Jennifer Calvert

ISBN 978-1-250-39640-2 (trade paperback)

The publisher of this book does not authorize the use or
reproduction of any part of this book in any manner for
the purpose of training artificial intelligence technologies
or systems. The publisher of this book expressly reserves
this book from the Text and Data Mining exception in
accordance with Article 4(3) of the European Union Digital
Single Market Directive 2019/790.

Our books may be purchased in bulk for specialty
retail/wholesale, literacy, corporate/premium, edu-
cational, and subscription box use. Please contact
MacmillanSpecialMarkets@macmillan.com.

First Edition: 2025

10 9 8 7 6 5 4 3 2 1

TAKE UP SPACE & CLAIM YOUR HAPPINESS

THE PEOPLE PLEASER'S RECOVERY JOURNAL

ELLIE SUMMERS

CASTLE POINT BOOKS
NEW YORK

YOU ARE THE MAIN CHARACTER

Sure thing!

To quote Kate Winslet (as Iris in *The Holiday*) mid-breakthrough, "You're supposed to be the leading lady in your own life!" In other words, you're the hero of this story. So it's time to stop acting like a supporting character who just pops into frame to nod and sip coffee. OK, the coffee can stay. But the masking, apologizing, approval-seeking, and putting everyone else first has got to go.

With a little help from your very own sidekick—*The People Pleaser's Recovery Journal*—you can take the lead and finally start living your life for *you*. Its prompts and advice will help you chisel through the layers of expectations and guilt to discover who you really are and what you actually want. You'll learn how to not only find your voice but also use it.

Of course!

People pleasers please people for any number of reasons, from anxiety and low self-esteem to social conditioning and childhood trauma. Journal exercises tailored to a few key areas can help you break out of old patterns and forge healthier ones:

Honesty
Be honest with yourself so you can be honest with others.

Empowerment
Gain the confidence to stand up for yourself (and sometimes *to* yourself).

Self-Care
Prioritize your needs so you can recognize when you're not doing so.

Boundaries
Learn how to draw lines and stand firmly behind them.

It's time for people to meet the real you. Don't worry—they'll like you. And if they don't, it won't matter, because *you'll* like you.

You're just a few short pages away from the freedom to be yourself!

Power is living your life on your own terms, how you want to, in a way that you feel good about.

KIRSTEN GREEN

CHECK YOUR MOTIVATION

Do you find yourself rushing through your morning yoga sessions or your afternoon lattes? Ask yourself why. Are you feeling guilty? Telling yourself you have more important things to do? Break down your rationale here.

Next time, remember this: you're worthy of taking this time for yourself—no justifications necessary.

CHOOSE YOU

Plan something wonderful just for you—whether that's a nail appointment, an afternoon of reading, or a fancy dinner. What will you do? When will you do it? How will it feel? Write it all out until you can taste that garlic butter.

Now put it on the calendar and prioritize it like you would a friend's birthday. By keeping your commitment to yourself, you train your brain to know that your needs matter.

When you say "yes" to others, make sure you aren't saying "no" to yourself.

PAULO COELHO

It's good to do uncomfortable things. It's weight training for life.

ANNE LAMOTT

BORROW SOME CONFIDENCE

Think back to a time when you wish you'd spoken up for yourself. (It probably wasn't that long ago.) Now channel your most confident friend and write out how they would have handled it.

HOT TIP: You can cosplay as your confident friend whenever you need to.

LEAN INTO THE AWKWARDNESS

A big reason for people-pleasing is to avoid the awkwardness of saying no. So start small: The next time you feel pressured to say yes to something trivial you'd rather not do, say no. Then breathe through the discomfort until it passes. What happened? How did you feel afterward?

Did the other person vow never to speak to you again? Of course not. Remember that the next time you find yourself squirming.

You wouldn't worry so much about what others think of you if you realized how seldom they do.

ELEANOR ROOSEVELT

If you're always trying to be normal, you will never know how amazing you can be.

MAYA ANGELOU

BREAK THE MOLD

Have you ever found yourself trying to "fit in"? (Who hasn't?) What would happen if you leaned into your unique quirks instead? How might your life feel freer or more authentic?

Being your true self isn't meant to be difficult, but people-pleasing makes it harder.

CLEAN HOUSE

Identify one negative belief or criticism you've been holding onto lately. Whose "dirty feet" brought it in? How can you evict this thought and reclaim your mental space?

It's their mud. Let them keep it.

I will not let anyone walk through my mind with their dirty feet.

MAHATMA GANDHI

> **Confidence is not "They will like me." Confidence instead is "I'll be fine if they don't."**

CHRISTINA GRIMMIE

KNOW YOUR OWN POWER

Write about a time when you stayed true to yourself even though it meant risking disapproval. How did it feel in the moment? How did it shape you?

Not everyone will agree with your choices. That doesn't mean they're right.

SET A BOUNDARY

What is something that irks you about someone in your life? Maybe it's how your mother-in-law drops by unannounced, or how your friend steals your fries. Write about why it annoys you, then declare your boundary (in writing—you can work up to saying it out loud).

Change begins with having the courage to tell your friend to get their own fries.

Courage is very important. Like a muscle, it is strengthened by use.

RUTH GORDON

> We must do our work for its own sake, not for fortune or attention or applause.

STEVEN PRESSFIELD

FOCUS ON THE PROCESS

What task or goal have you been pursuing? If no one noticed or praised you for it, would you still find meaning in it? Be honest! If it's a yes, how can you find more joy in the process?

If it's a no, why are you doing it? Give yourself permission to let it go.

BE UNAPOLOGETIC IN YOUR JOY

What's your "guiltiest" pleasure? *Real Housewives*? Pricey cheese? The fact that "MMMBop" is on your playlist? Write about why it brings you joy and how you can embrace it unapologetically this week.

Comparison is the thief of joy—don't let other people's opinions steal your joy.

I don't believe in guilty pleasures. If you enjoy something, there's nothing guilty about it.

BUSY PHILIPPS

> One day a long time from now you'll cease to care anymore whom you please or what anybody has to say about you. That's when you'll finally produce the work you're capable of.

J. D. SALINGER

REVEL IN YOUR FREEDOM

Imagine your future self, fully confident and free from the need to please others. What are you doing differently? Write a letter of advice from future you to present you, encouraging you to take bold steps.

HINT: This is as much about trusting yourself as it is about reshaping your life.

REDEFINE RESPECT

Whose feelings do you tend to prioritize over your own? Are they really worth the effort, or are you inching into martyrdom territory? How can you clarify those standards of respect—both yours and theirs?

Some people will be worth the effort—but not everyone.

If you spend your life sparing people's feelings and feeding their vanity, you get so you can't distinguish what *should* be respected in them.

F. SCOTT FITZGERALD

We have to be willing to fail, to be wrong, to start over again with lessons learned.

ANGELA LEE DUCKWORTH

REFRAME YOUR MISTAKES

People pleasers are particularly hard on themselves when they make mistakes. But no one is perfect. What are some mistakes you've seen loved ones make? Did it make you think any less of them?

The next time you're beating yourself up, remember this and give yourself the same compassion you give others.

PRIORITIZE YOUR DREAMS

Are other people trying to talk you out of following your dreams (or just from enjoying yourself)? Are you letting them? Why?

Odds are good it won't be as bad as you fear. And you can handle a little side-eye.

Go after what it is that creates meaning in your life and then trust yourself to handle the stress that follows.

KELLY McGONIGAL

If two men agree on everything, you may be sure that one of them is doing the thinking.

LYNDON B. JOHNSON

WELCOME THE FRICTION

Think about a time when you benefitted from constructive criticism or honest feedback. How was it helpful?

Not pleasing people may be uncomfortable sometimes, but that friction has value—it helps you grow toward yourself.

KNOW YOUR OWN STRENGTH

What are some things you've done in your life that have been difficult but rewarding? From opening that tricky jar of pickles to moving to a new town, it all counts.

REMEMBER THIS: You've done harder things than set boundaries.

Discomfort is the price of admission to a meaningful life.

SUSAN DAVID

Perfect is overrated. Perfect is boring.

STEPHANIE PERKINS

CELEBRATE IMPERFECTION

Perfectionism goes hand in hand with people-pleasing. But our imperfections are part of us—sometimes the best part. Think about your closest friends. Which of their imperfections do you love? Why?

No one you know is perfect. Better still, no one you like is perfect.

LET YOURSELF DREAM

Take some time to daydream. What's important to you? What do you like? What do you want to do?

There shouldn't be any "shoulds" on this page! (Other than these two.)

SELF-CARE SELF-CARE SELF-CARE SELF-CARE SELF-CARE

We must give ourselves permission to be who we want to be, even if we don't have the blueprint yet, and that starts with dreaming.

LUVVIE AJAYI JONES

It actually doesn't take much to be considered a difficult woman. That's why there's so many of us.

JANE GOODALL

EMBRACE THE LABEL

When has being "difficult" (aka standing up for yourself) helped you get what you need?

Whether you need to leave a toxic job or just ask a waiter for a fork, know that it's OK to be "difficult."

OWN YOUR EDGE

How do your "thorns" (boundaries) protect you or make you stronger?
How have you blossomed because of them?

You're not being prickly when you set boundaries—you're
showing people you're worthy of respect.

Your thorns are the best part of you.

MARIANNE MOORE

We weren't born distrusting and fearing ourselves. That was part of our taming.

GLENNON DOYLE

BE UNTAMED

What would you be capable of doing if you could shake the nagging feeling that someone might judge you for doing it? (Barring anything illegal or immoral, of course.)

This isn't middle school—you're not being graded. Go for it!

REWRITE THE RULES

What "rule" have you been following that doesn't actually serve you? What's one way you can break that rule this week to bring more joy and freedom into your life?

HOT TIP: This is your life. You make the rules.

If you obey all the rules, you miss all the fun.

KATHARINE HEPBURN

It's not enough to be nice in life. You've got to have nerve.

GEORGIA O'KEEFFE

BE BOLD

Think of a situation in which being "nice" didn't get you anywhere. Would you have been better off taking a bold approach? How so?

Honey is sweet, but it's not always effective.
Sometimes, you catch more flies with fly traps.

FREE UP YOUR TIME

What's on your to-do list that you'd rather scratch off? How would that free you up for something better? Is it worth a try?

Save your yes for the things that feel most aligned with who you want to be.

When we step up for ourselves, we create opportunity.

KERRY WASHINGTON

Your time is limited, so don't waste it living someone else's life.

STEVE JOBS

NOTICE THE "SHOULDS"

As you go through your day, consider how often you're doing what you want to be doing and how often you're doing what you think you *should* be doing. What did you discover? Anything you'd like to change?

How about trading that kale smoothie for a toaster pastry tomorrow? It's called balance.

CREATE A BRIGHT SPOT

How can you protect your joy today? What can you do right now that will make you happy regardless of whatever else is going on in your life? Come back and revel in it when you're done.

_____
_____
_____
_____
_____
_____
_____
_____
_____
_____
_____
_____
_____
_____
_____
_____

Even if you can't shake your people-pleasing ways today, you can devote a few moments to your own happiness.

SELF-CARE SELF-CARE SELF-CARE SELF-CARE SELF-CARE

How are you protecting your joy each day? Because in joy we see even darkness with new eyes.

VALARIE KAUR

If it's a good idea, go ahead and do it. It's easier to ask forgiveness than it is to get permission.

GRACE HOPPER

DO THE THING

Have you ever gotten the idea to do something and just *did* it? Without asking for anyone's opinion beforehand? How did it feel? If not, what is something you'd like to do without getting others' permission or approval?

If you haven't yet, do it now. You may just discover a new superpower.

SHOW SOME RESPECT

How can you show respect for your own time, feelings, and intrinsic value? It might look like keeping a promise to yourself, having a good cry if you need one, walking away from a bad situation, or something entirely unique to you.

REMEMBER: You don't have to provide value to be of value.

Deal with yourself as an individual worthy of respect, and make everyone else deal with you the same way.

NIKKI GIOVANNI

You can't be hesitant about who you are.

VIOLA DAVIS

GET TO KNOW YOURSELF

Who are you? What do you believe in? What do you like? Write a short bio that describes what makes you *you*.

Use this description as a compass rose when you're making decisions, and you'll be less likely to let others' opinions steer you off-course.

FIND YOUR CENTER

What's something that calms and centers you? Do you like to color or knit? Do you love going to the movies alone? How can you incorporate more of that relaxing activity into your life?

Focus at least some of that people-pleasing energy inward.

Trying to please everybody is impossible— if you did that, you'd end up in the middle with nobody liking you.

JOHN LENNON

Spend less time tearing yourself apart, worrying if you're good enough. You are good enough.

REESE WITHERSPOON

BE PROUD OF YOURSELF

When do you feel most dynamic and powerful? When do you feel least sure of yourself? What's the difference? What would help you bring a little of that self-assuredness to all you do?

People-pleasing often comes from a place of insecurity. Appreciate how much you bring to the table. (Hint: It's a lot.)

RAISE THE BAR

Most of the time, you set the bar. Where do you need to raise it? In what ways are your needs not being met?

Find small ways to inch that bar higher until it's where you need it to be.

The minute you settle for less than you deserve, you get even less than you settled for.

MAUREEN DOWD

Define success on your own terms, achieve it by your own rules, and build a life you're proud to live.

ANNE SWEENEY

RETHINK THE MEANING OF SUCCESS

How do *you* define success? While you're writing, try to filter out anything that feels suspiciously like other people's opinions, societal expectations, or self-imposed obligations.

That desire to please can be sneaky. The more you notice it, the less pull it will have over you.

EXPRESS YOURSELF

What's something you love that you're willing to go to the mat for? Whether it's bacon on doughnuts, a favorite TV show, or volunteering for a nonprofit, describe what you love about it. Then think about how you can bring more of that passion into your life.

Being inspired by others is great, but we all need a passion that's uniquely ours.

Most people are other people. Their thoughts are someone else's opinions, their lives a mimicry, their passions a quotation.

OSCAR WILDE

Courage doesn't always roar. Sometimes courage is the quiet voice at the end of the day saying, "I will try again tomorrow."

MARY ANNE RADMACHER

TRY, TRY AGAIN

How do you feel after you've given into your people-pleasing ways? How can you learn from that feeling? How might you go about the situation next time?

Don't beat yourself up—change takes time, and being willing to change takes guts. You've got plenty of both.

FOCUS ON GOOD FRIENDS

Think about people in your life who are particularly negative and hard to please. Then think about people who are especially supportive. How can you redirect your energy to the latter group?

_____
_____
_____
_____
_____
_____
_____
_____
_____
_____
_____
_____
_____
_____

Spend your energy on the people who've earned it.

No person is your friend who demands your silence, or denies your right to grow.

ALICE WALKER

Don't let you be the reason why you're not advancing or becoming who you want to be.

JOANNE S. BASS

TAKE RESPONSIBILITY

Think about the last time other people's opinions stopped you short. Was it really them? Or was it you? Did you let your own worries get in your way?

At the end of the day, the only person stopping you from doing what you want is you. (In most things. Paying your bills is, sadly, not optional.)

HYPE YOURSELF UP

List all of the many amazing things about yourself, from your kind smile to your mouthwatering pasta recipe. Try to fill up every bit of open space on the page.

What others think of you matters a whole lot less when you're secure in what you bring to the table.

The most powerful relationship you will ever have is the relationship with yourself.

STEVE MARABOLI

Self-esteem comes from being able to define the world in your own terms and refusing to abide by the judgments of others.

OPRAH WINFREY

TAKE A BEAT

The next time you're feeling the pressure from someone, take a beat. Come back to this page and ask yourself: *What's my gut telling me? What do I really want?*

Learning to listen to your own voice is life-changing.

AGREE TO DISAGREE

Think about a time when you've disagreed with someone but kept your opinion to yourself. Why did you keep quiet? What do you think would have happened if you'd expressed yourself?

There's nothing wrong with picking your battles, but there's also nothing wrong with letting people know where you stand. In fact, it can help them feel closer to you.

Don't be afraid of losing people, but be afraid of losing yourself trying to make everyone happy.

NAGUIB MAHFOUZ

The price we pay for being ourselves is worth it.

EARTHA KITT

CREATE STRONGER RELATIONSHIPS

How has being true to you helped you find new friends? How has it helped you deepen your connection with others?

Your people are the ones with whom you don't have to mask or minimize or pretend to laugh at their terrible jokes (because you'll actually laugh at their terrible jokes).

POWER UP

People-pleasing burnout is a real problem. What can you do to recharge your battery? How can you make sure it doesn't get critically low again?

Only you know how much you have to give, and only you pay the price if you give too much.

Self-care is how you take your power back.

LALAH DELIA

Doubt kills more dreams than failure ever will.

SUZY KASSEM

MAKE YOUR ARGUMENT

What's something you want that others might push back on? Write out an argument that would convince your toughest critic (you).

Whether people have your best interests at heart or not doesn't actually matter. Your resolve has to be stronger than your desire to placate them.

USE YOUR VOICE

Think about small ways you wish you'd used your voice in the past, from ordering takeout over the phone, to saying "I can't today" to a friend, to respectfully disagreeing with a coworker. Turn it into a checklist for the future.

The more you do it, the easier it gets. Then suddenly, one day, it'll be second nature.

It took me quite a long time to develop a voice, and now that I have it, I am not going to be silent.

MADELEINE ALBRIGHT

Your need for acceptance can make you invisible in this world.... Risk being seen in all of your glory.

JIM CARREY

STEP INTO THE SPOTLIGHT

People-pleasing isn't the only way to get approval and acceptance. How might you feel that warmth while being true to yourself?

HINT: Just think about the compliments you've received over the years.

PROTECT YOUR PEACE

Before you say yes to the next thing, come here and list everything else on your to-do list. Then ask yourself: *Do I really have the bandwidth for more?* Even better: *Can I find any ways to lighten my load?*

You're no good to anyone—particularly yourself—if you're in a constant state of overwhelm.

Giving up doesn't always mean you're weak. Sometimes you're just strong enough to let go.

TAYLOR SWIFT

You can never leave footprints that last if you are always walking on tiptoe.

LEYMAH GBOWEE

MAKE PEACE WITH CONFLICT

What do you hope to accomplish in your life? Is it possible to do it all while also pleasing everyone? (No. The answer is no.) Is it worth fighting for?

Conflict is inevitable, so the best you can do is choose which hills you're willing to die on.

INSPIRE OTHERS

Boundaries cut both ways. Have you offered your help or opinion without being asked for it? What could you have done differently to model healthy boundaries to others?

_____
_____
_____
_____
_____
_____
_____
_____
_____
_____
_____
_____
_____
_____
_____

And when someone comes to you with their own unsolicited opinions, a simple, self-assured, "Thanks, but I got this," can work wonders.

BOUNDARIES BOUNDARIES BOUNDARIESS BOUNDARIE

Don't let people pull you into their storm. Pull them into your peace.

PEMA CHÖDRÖN

Happiness comes from being who you actually are instead of who you think you are supposed to be.

SHONDA RHIMES

YOU DO YOU

When have you been at your happiest? What were you doing? Were you being true to yourself in those moments, or were you following someone else's lead?

Sure, being inspired by your neighbor to try yoga can lead to happiness. Being guilted into doing it, though? Not so much.

ACCEPT THE MESS

How do you tidy yourself up for others? (Figuratively or literally—both count.) Do you soften your edges? Do you think they'd like you less if you let loose? Why?

Everyone is messy in one way or another. Yes, even the people who post their spotless kitchens on social media.

Embrace the glorious mess that you are.

ELIZABETH GILBERT

> There's no map for you to follow and take your journey. You are Lewis and Clark. You are the mapmaker.
>
> **PHILLIPA SOO**

CHART YOUR OWN COURSE

How can you start carving out your own path, apart from what you feel others (parents, teachers, society, etc.) have laid out for you? What would it look like?

You're in charge of who you ask for directions and whether you follow them.

BE KIND, NOT JUST NICE

What do you think is the difference between being kind and being nice? Which one matters more to you? Are there areas where you need to make a swap?

If you think they're synonymous, dig deeper.

If someone calls you bossy because you didn't let them push you around, so be it.

MARY BARRA

Your true self is right there, buried under cultural conditioning, other people's opinions, and inaccurate conclusions you drew as a kid that became your beliefs about who you are.

EMILY MCDOWELL

NOTICE YOUR PATTERNS

List a few of your core beliefs. Where did they come from? Trace them back to their roots. Are they still serving you well? Why or why not?

HOT TIP: You can change your beliefs any time you want!

VALIDATE YOURSELF

What are some ways you can validate your own opinions and actions when you're tempted to turn to others? Come up with a go-to list.

They can have opinions, but they don't get a vote.

The only approval you need is your own.

AMANDA GORMAN

I'm not dimming my light. I'm just gonna hand you some shades.

LISA NICHOLS

SHINE YOUR LIGHT

Think about a time when you've dimmed your light to help others feel brighter. Did they need you to do that? How might shining brightly have helped them more?

Be a towering lighthouse, not a light bulb with a dimmer switch.

KNOW WHEN TO WALK AWAY

Looking back, were there people or situations you should have walked away from? Those that didn't deserve your presence, energy, and effort. How can you honor that lesson now?

No one is entitled to have you in their life—not even relatives. They have to earn it.

You've got to learn to leave the table when love's no longer being served.

NINA SIMONE

No matter what I do, I ask myself three questions: What do I want? Why do I want it? And how do I get it?

STACEY ABRAMS

ASK YOURSELF WHY

What's something you really want for yourself? To buy a home? To move to Spain? To start jogging? Why do you want it? Get into the weeds of it.

Understanding the "why" can help you prioritize what you want or, sometimes, help you realize you don't actually want it.

BE TOO MUCH

When have you been made to feel like you're "too much"?
When have you been embraced by people for being authentically you?
Found people genuinely willing to help you? Which of these groups of
people do you respect more, and why?

Your needs are your needs. If someone feels they're too much, that's usually a "them problem."

It's never overreacting to ask for what you want and need.

AMY POEHLER

Go out there and do something remarkable. Don't live down to expectations.

WENDY WASSERSTEIN

TAKE THE LEAD

How can you lean into your newfound main-character energy? What can you do to step out of the box you've put yourself in for so long?

Baby steps count!

SKIP THE APOLOGY

How often do you apologize? Does every email response that took longer than five minutes start with "Sorry!"? Do you excuse yourself after bumping into inanimate objects? How can you reframe some of those apologies? (For example, you could say "Thanks for waiting" instead of "Sorry I'm late.")

Your time and space are just as valid as anyone else's (including that coat rack you bumped into). Reinforce that fact by avoiding unnecessary apologies.

> We need to step into our power and not give it over to anyone or apologize for it.

VIOLA DAVIS

One of the most courageous things you can do is identify yourself, know who you are, what you believe in, and where you want to go.

SHIELA MURRAY BETHEL

DECIDE WHO YOU ARE

Now that you've had some practice and done the work, who do you want to be? Write about that person.

It gets a lot easier to say no to others when you're clear on what you want from yourself.

We always may be what we might have been.

ADELAIDE ANNE PROCTER